Plants For Fruit Guilds

By Kathryn Robles

Copyright © 2020 Kathryn Robles
All rights reserved.

Table of Contents

Plants For Fruit Guilds i
How To Start A Fruit Tree Guild 2
Purposes Of Fruit Tree Guilds 4
Most Popular Plants For Fruit Guilds 12
The Best Plants To Suppress Grass Around Fruit Trees 16
55 Trees That Are Great For Fruit Tree Guilds 19
Vines You Should Grow in Your Fruit Tree Guild 23
16 Great Ground Covers For Your Fruit Tree Guild 28
44 Insectiary Plants For Your Fruit Tree Guild 33
What Are The Best Nitrogen Fixers? 36
17 Dynamic Accumulators You Need In Your Food Forest 44
Best Plants To Chop and Drop In Your Fruit Tree Guild 47
The Most Common Challenges To Starting A Fruit Tree Guild 53

How To Start A Fruit Tree Guild

Instead of planting an orchard in traditional rows, you may want to consider planting a fruit tree guild! A fruit tree guild is like companion plants for your fruit trees. The different plants work together to feed each other, repel bad bugs and disease, and attract pollinators.

By adding a fruit tree guild around each of your fruit trees or bushes you can grow more food in a smaller area. This is particularly good for urban homesteaders because we don't have much space to work with. Every little bit counts!

When you create communities of plants that benefit each other you can reduce disease and increase your harvests, all with less work on your part. The plants in a guild work together to recycle nutrients back into the soil, save water, provide shade, attract beneficial insects and prevent erosion. And they do all this while providing food, flowers, and medicine for us as well.

Many people are familiar with the idea of companion plants in the vegetable garden. Fruit tree guilds are based on the same idea. It's like tomatoes and basil, or corn, beans, and squash, but for your apples and pears.

Permaculture uses the forest as its guide in how to fill different roles with plants. Forests grow in layers, and there are a total of eight. First you have your canopy layer, which is your tallest trees that need the most sun.

Then you have your understory trees. These do fine with a bit of shade.

Next is the shrub layer, which is bushes and plants around three to six feet tall. The herbaceous layer is herbs and greens. The groundcover layer includes grass, but also many different groundcover plants. The underground layer is filled with roots. Then mixed in among those layers you also have your climbing plants as well as your fungi.

As you can see, forests have a lot going on! Each of these different layers and plants fill different needs and roles. What's better is that you don't have to stop at just one fruit tree guild. You can combine individual guilds into a larger guild to build a food forest as well as provide wildlife habitat.

Purposes Of Fruit Tree Guilds

The beautiful thing about guilds is that they fill so many different roles. They can attract pollinators, discourage bad bugs, add to the fertility of your land, deter wildlife, provide privacy, and even save water. And that isn't even including the food you'll produce for yourself!

By planting species that fulfill each of these roles you can grow fruit trees that will continually improve the soil and your land each year. You can even choose plants that fill more than one role at a time to really increase your land's productivity.

Pollinators

A common purpose for plants in a fruit tree guild is to attract pollinators. Choose host plants that provide nectar or pollen. Whenever possible, choose plants that are in bloom when your fruit tree will be.

In addition to attracting the "good bugs," also choose plants that repel or confuses harmful insects. (Marigolds are commonly used for this purpose in vegetable gardens). You can also choose plants that will attract birds as well.

If you're not sure how to start, observe what types of pests you have in your yard currently. What beneficial insects eat those types of pests? Once you know what insects you need to attract, find out which species will help draw them to your fruit trees and other plants.

Increase Fertility

Nitrogen fixers are plants that move nitrogen from the air and into the soil. Plants require nitrogen to grow, and the common solution is to feed them fertilizer. However, if you plant nitrogen fixers, you are essentially growing your own fertilizer for free.

Nitrogen fixers host bacteria called Rhizobium. These bacteria take the nitrogen gas and converts it to a nodule on the rotos of the plant. When the plant dies and begins to decompose this nitrogen is released into the soil where other plants can use it.

Dynamic accumulators are also essential. This group of plants most often has long deep roots that can access minerals and nutrients deep within the soil. It accumulates those nutrients in its leaves and stems, and then when it dies and decomposes the minerals are returned to the soil.

Plants with long tap roots are also good for aerating and breaking up dense soils. When they are pulled up or decompose the oxygen is beneficial and the soil structure is improved.

Both dynamic accumulators and nitrogen fixers make good mulch plants. Cut mulch plants back and let the decompose in place in order to provide nutrients and cover. Just as a forest floor is constantly replenishing itself with fallen leaves, we should provide the same cover for our mini forests. A layer of mulch protects your topsoil and retains water, as well as supporting necessary microorganisms.

Influence Wildlife

Guilds can also be useful in attracting or detracting wildlife. Planting many different species can attract birds and butterflies and all manner of interesting creatures. On the other hand, you may wish to discourage some that are less desirable. One enterprising permaculturist used a double-sided guild as a hedgerow. One side was thickly planted with plants attractive to deer. The deer would eat along the hedge row until they were directed away from the property. However, the inside of the hedgerow was plants for humans to harvest!

You can also use your guilds to provide plenty of food for your own flock of chickens or herd of rabbits. Just be aware that chickens can be very destructive so don't let them free range until your plants get well established.

Shade and Privacy

Fruit trees also give ambient benefits by providing shade, beauty, and privacy. They improve the aesthetics of your land and can be quite attractive to look at. The mix of plants in your guilds should certainly include ornamentals. Just because you are growing your own food doesn't mean it can't be beautiful as well.

You can use guilds to provide a screen between you and your neighbors or plant a thick hedge to slow down cold winds. Planting lots of trees on the north side of your house can cool down the ambient temperatures of your property without shading south facing summer vegetables.

Guilds are great for all types of plants, natives, perennials, and annuals. If you have a bare spot that you want to be more attractive, throw some annual flowers into it while the other plants grow.

Food and Medicine

And of course, our fruit tree guilds provide food for us as well. Not only do we want the delicious fruits from our main tree, but we can choose plants for around it that provide other crops. We can grow berries, greens, even mushrooms!

Many pollinator friendly plants also have herbal benefits. You can grow your own medicines and herbal remedies while at the same time supporting the health of your backyard orchard.

How To Start A Fruit Tree Guild

With all these benefits, how exactly do you go about planting a fruit tree guild? First, decide what you want your central tree to be. Popular choices are apples, pears, plums, nuts, et cetera. Any large tree or bush can be the center of your guild.

Pick fruit trees that do well in your climate. One strategy for finding out what grows well is checking out farmers markets and seeing which produce is available. Your county extension office also should be able to recommend good varieties.

Maps of hardiness zones should be able to get you pointed in the right direction as well. Some trees require chill hours. This means that it needs a certain number of hours under 45 degrees before it bears fruit. Most apples don't grow well in warm places (like Texas!) for this reason.

Next you can consider the micro-climate of your property. Consider where power lines and sewer lines run. Chat with the neighbors before you plant something that will hang over your property line or interfere with a fence.

Observe how the sun moves across your property and what parts need more shade, or already have shade. Planting a tree can change that microclimate, so make sure you consider the effect on shade and wind the full-grown tree will have.

Also examine your soil. Do you have parts of your yard that are very dry? How about some that tend to have standing water after a storm? If you have any sloped land, then the tops of your slopes will stay warmer than the bottoms. This may be very useful in choosing where to plant a heat loving citrus versus an apple that needs those chilly winters.

Don't forget to consider space for paths. Planning ahead for paths is probably the most common mistake that people make when planting their food forests. It's hard to imagine these tiny trees fully grown and they often are planted too close together.

Next, it's time to pick what plants to include in your fruit guild! This is probably the most fun, but also the most complicated part of starting a fruit tree guild. You'll want to include each of the different layers. Pick one tree for your overstory layer. If you have space add smaller trees for the understory layer. Next add your small fruits, shrubs, or bushes. Finally, fill in with herbs, greens, vines, ground covers, and fungi.

You'll want to consider the different rooting habits of each of the plants. If you have a fruit tree that is shallow rooted keep other surface feeders away from its root zone. You'll also want to suppress grass from growing around the tree.

While grass can be nice to walk on if you have kids, it is not a good companion for fruit trees. It competes for nutrients. Also, grass requires frequent watering, while your fruit trees should have less frequent watering for longer periods of time. You can plant bulbs that provide a physical barrier or groundcover that will keep the grass from getting established.

To plant your fruit tree guild, plant your center tree, and mark its adult size. The edge of this measurement is called the drip line. Start about 6 to 12 inches from the trunk and place cardboard out to the drip line all around the tree. Cover the cardboard with soil or compost. If you can let this break down for a bit before planting it can help your other plants get established.

Now it's time to add in your other plants. Make sure to include your ring of bulbs to keep the grass out of your newly prepared bed. Many of the plants commonly used also discourage rabbits and deer. When you plant vining plants, give them a support other than the tree trunk as well.

Exactly how you group your plants is up to you. Keep in mind you want to create a mini ecosystem. You'll want to include plants that grow well together and have multiple uses. You can observe which plants naturally grow together in wild situations. Pick pollinator plants that bloom when your tree will be in bloom or that fill a specific nutrient need your tree may have.

There are very few wrong choices when it comes to tree guilds. If a plant isn't doing well, you can always try adding other plants to see if you get a better match. Even if you don't get your guild perfect the first time around, this is a great way to increase the health of your fruit trees and increase the beauty and production level of your property.

Most Popular Plants For Fruit Guilds

When you are planning out a fruit tree guild you can use any plants you want, but there are some plants that are used quite frequently. The best plants are those that have multiple uses, especially if they are also a food crop.

Put the most food crops you can in the least amount of space. Here are some great edible crops to include:

- Apples
- Arugula
- Artichokes
- Asparagus
- Blackberry
- Buckwheat
- Chives
- Currants
- Dill
- Echinacea
- Edible Honeysuckle
- Fennel
- Garlic
- Ginseng
- Gooseberry
- Hazel/Filberts
- Hosta

- Hyssop
- Oregano
- Pear
- Peppermint
- Quince
- Raspberry
- Rhubarb
- Rugosa rose
- Thyme

There are some popular plants that are almost always included in a food forest because they are so useful, even though they are not grown for food. Here are some of the top ones!

- Clover
- Comfrey
- False Indigo
- Geranium
- Lucerne
- Queen Anne's Lace

The Layers of a Food Forest

When you plant a food forest, it is common to mimic a naturally occurring food forest and to grow different layers of plants. You have your very tall tree layer, followed by an understory tree layer.

Growing throughout all the layers will be the vine layer, which takes advantage of the available vertical space. Next up is the shrub layer. The shrub layer can reach up to six feet tall and join in the understory layer depending on how large your plants grow.

Popular plants to include in this layer are roses, serviceberry, filberts, willow, bamboo, butter y bush, lilac, raspberry, chokeberry, cherry dogwood, elder, sage, and rosemary.

The next layer is the herb layer. There is a large variety of plants that can be included here. Many nitrogen fixers belong in the herb layer, as do dynamic accumulators.

Some other good choices for the herb layer are sweet cicely, parsley, tarragon, fennel, dill, thyme, peppers, tomatoes, okra, collards, Good King Henry, chard, bush beans, echinacea, mint, chives, and lemongrass.

After the herb layer, you'll want to include some ground covers. And while you may not be able to see it, you can also include root crops in your food forest! Popular plants for this layer include daikon radish, turnips, potatoes, sunchokes, turmeric, ginger, carrots, parsnips, garlic, onions, sweet potato, and licorice.

Other types of plants for your food forest

Just because a plant isn't edible doesn't mean that it doesn't have a place in your fruit tree guilds or food forest. Sometimes you may want to include plants for medicinal purposes, or to help keep the other plants healthier. For example, foxglove is poisonous, however it can be a great "plant doctor" and prevent problems to the plants around it.

You may also want to include barrier or hedge plants or consider including a windbreak. Spiney plants such as boxthorn, pyracantha or acacia armata can be planted around new trees to protect them from chicken damage. Euphorbia can successfully deter moles and other burrowing vermin.

There are also good reasons to include livestock in your fruit tree guilds as well. For example, chickens eat apple parasites and geese keep grass under control. Not to mention poultry can be great for soil fertility. Just make sure everything is well established first!

Whether you include the most popular plants in your fruit tree guild, or opt for something a little more untypical, including a variety of plants in your food forest will help it be strong, healthier, and more productive.

The Best Plants To Suppress Grass Around Fruit Trees

If you want to have the best producing fruit trees, it's important to keep competing plants away from your backyard orchard. There are a couple ways to suppress grass in your fruit tree guild.

Traditionally orchards consist of trees in rows, with grass in between. This makes it easy for large equipment to pass between the rows, but it isn't ideal for the health of the tree.

A better option is to suppress grass up to the drip line of your fruit trees so that the roots aren't competing for nutrients. (The drip line is the edge of the leaves and will increase each year as your tree grows). Instead of rows, imagine your trees as connected by concentric circles.

Under the canopy, you can lay down mulch and plant beneficial and useful plants that won't compete with your tree's root system. Grass is a major weed however, and it will try to creep in. An easy solution is to plant grass suppressing plants at the edge of the tree.

Plants That Suppress Grass

Some of the best grass suppressing plants also have other uses. Whenever you can get multiple uses out of the same plant do it! It will save you space and time!

Chives
Chives are a great option because they are useful in the kitchen as a garnish or spice. They add a nice mild flavor and are great for things such as egg dishes.

Chives also produce attractive flowers that are good for beneficial insects. Plus, chives will come back year after year for you!

Irises
You can't eat irises, and they only bloom in the spring, but boy are they pretty! Irises are a great plant for front yard fruit tree guilds because they are a traditional ornamental flower. They also multiply easily, so you can propagate your own and share with friends.

I currently have irises in my yard in San Antonio that came from my grandmother's house in Utah, to my uncle's house in Oregon, to my house in Oregon, and finally to my house here in San Antonio. These are the best sort of keepsake!

Daffodils
Like irises, daffodils are kind of a one trick pony. They are also poisonous, so don't eat them! They're great for suppressing grass in the early spring though, when it grows the most quickly.

Plus, if you plant daffodils, tulips, and irises in the same area you can have non-stop blooms all spring.

Daylilies

Daylilies are another attractive flower, and these can be edible too! The tuber can be dried and eaten. (Just don't mistake it for a true lily, which grows from a bulb, not a tuber.)

Garlic

Garlic is one of my FAVORITE things to grow. Probably because it's one of the few things I don't kill! Garlic is super easy to grow. Plus, it's super useful in the kitchen, and just about everybody knows how to use it.

It's also a great option for around your fruit trees because it attracts beneficial insects AND repels the noxious ones!

Leeks

A relative of both chives and garlic is leeks. This tall member of the onion family makes a handsome addition to fruit tree guilds with its large attractive flowers.

It comes with all the benefits of chives and garlic. Plus, it can be grown from scraps and then planted into your garden. That's a win for homesteading on a budget!

Grow some of these plants around the edges of your fruit trees to suppress grass. They will keep competing weeds out with little work on your part, look attractive, and attract useful pollinators!

55 Trees That Are Great For Fruit Tree Guilds

The central part of fruit tree guilds is the fruit tree! You don't actually need a *fruit* tree for a guild, however. And sometimes including other trees is a good option too. Here is a mega list of 55 trees that grow well in a forest garden.

Central Trees For Fruit Tree Guilds

Generally, guilds are planned out with one tree in the center, and other understory trees, bushes, herbs, and groundcovers radiating out from the center. Your central trees tend to be taller than other trees, and they generally need full sun.

Here are some great options for you. Most of these trees do produce an edible crop. Some are good for herbal medicine. Others are beautiful additions to your landscape and good for the surrounding ecosystem.

While central trees do tend to grow quite large, if you only have a small yard, consider choosing a dwarf rootstock variety instead.

- Alder
- Almond
- Apples
- Avocado
- Black Locust

- Carob
- Chestnuts
- Crabapple
- Date Palm
- Linden
- Macadamia
- Mango
- Medlar
- Mesquite
- Mulberry
- Nut-Bearing Pines
- Pears
- Pecan
- Plum
- Quince
- Robe Locust
- Silver Birch
- Tagasaste
- Walnuts

Understory Trees For Your Food Forest

In addition to a central leader tree, fruit tree guilds thrive with understory trees. Just make sure to give all the trees enough elbow room when you plant them!

Some trees are happy as a central leader or an understory tree in their food forest! Most understory

trees do ne with a little bit of shade, although they will fruit better with more sun.
- Almond
- Apricot
- Asian Pear
- Cacao
- Carambola (Star Fruit)
- Cherry
- Citrus
- Co ee
- Damson
- Dwarf Apple
- Elderberry
- Feijoa (Pineapple Guava)
- Fig
- Greengage
- Guava
- Hawthorn (Mayflower)
- Hazelnut
- Jujube (Chinese Date)
- Laburnum (Golden Chain Tree) *Poisonous but good for pollinators*
- Loquat
- Medlar
- Mulberry and Black Mulberry
- Nectarine
- Olive

- Papaya
- Pawpaw
- Peach
- Pear
- Pecan
- Persimmon
- Plum
- Pomegranate
- Rowan (mountain ash)
- Serviceberry
- Siberian Pea Shrub

Vines You Should Grow in Your Fruit Tree Guild

After you get your trees planted it's time to start adding other layers in your food forest. The vine layer is a great way of maximizing your space and adding in more crops in less space.

Vines can sometimes compete with trees for nutrients and can choke the trunk, so make sure to provide separate scaffolding for your vines. They can still be grown near your trees, however.

Good places to put vines include near fences and rain barrels, and up pergola and patio supports. If you have none of those it's pretty easy to create your own simple trellis.

11 Vines You Should Grow
Clematis

Clematis is a popular flowering vine because it has beautiful flowers and is perennial. It's a member of the buttercup family and is not edible, but it is a food source for some caterpillars, and it does attract birds.

Different varieties bloom at different times, so you could plant a variety to make sure you have constant flowers through the growing season. The different varieties also different sizes, and smaller varieties can be grown in containers.

The plant prefers sun, but roots like to stay cool. Keep it well mulched and plant a shorter companion plant to shade the roots. It can be planted in the fall or in early spring. While it does climb, it can also be used as a ground cover.

Cucumbers

Cucumbers are annuals, but they do make nice additions to your vertical space. They can be grown on the ground but are easily trained up a trellis. They are happy in a pot or in a sunny patch of the yard.

Cucumbers would be a good choice for young food forests because there will be plenty of sun, and you can plant it in spaces where more permanent plants will grow into in future years.

Grapes

Grapes are delicious and make beautiful vines. They also can grow well on hills and in poorer soil, which makes them perfect for those spaces where you can't puy anything else.

They're also great for privacy along property lines or to shade a patio or arbor. They will need strong support, and they will last for several years, so make sure you're happy with where you planted them.

Honeysuckle

While honeysuckle can be called edible, it isn't a food crop. Its wonderful scent and attractive flowers still makes it a valuable member of a food forest.

Honeysuckle is ideal for hiding rain barrels or other homestead features, and it also is lovely planted outside windows. When you open the window, you get a cool breeze and its delicate scent.

Hops

Hops are traditionally used in flavoring beer and also have some medicinal uses. They also have attractive foliage and grow quickly. They are ideal for shade and for those interested in homebrewing.

Kiwi

While many people think of kiwi as a tropical fruit, there are hardy varieties that can grow in more chilly climates. The vines can grow quite large, and you will need at least two, a male and a female.

There are self-pollinating varieties out there, but you'll want to double check before purchasing just one. They'll also need a sturdy trellis as they can get quite heavy with a full crop of fruit on them.

Melons

Like cucumbers, you can squish melons pretty much anywhere in a young food forest. They will need full sun and will be perfectly happy on the ground or on a trellis.

Just make sure to provide support for the fruit so they don't break off.

Passionflower

Passion flower is a tropical vine, so if you live in a colder area you will need to grow them as an annual. They may even be able to make it through winter with a deep mulch. It's easy to grow and is a good food source for butterflies.

They like full sun, although in very hot climates, they won't mind a bit of afternoon shade.

Pole Beans

Pole beans are a smaller vining plant and an annual. They are ideal for tucking into smaller corners to maximize your total growing space. They do great in container gardens with other veggies.

You can even grow them as companion plants for the classic bean, corn and squash triad. And if you have more space, you can easily grow your own years' worth of green beans for the freezer.

Rambling and climbing roses

Roses are one of my all-time favorite flowers. They can be time intensive to grow and need a bit more care than some plants, but generally the wild varieties that climb are much more hardy.

Rose hips make a tasty tea, the flowers are beautiful, and climbing roses will add quite the element of charm and whimsy to your food forest. They are perfectly suited for front yard gardens.

Squashes

As an annual, squash are a great filler plant. I used squash to fill in empty spaces in the landscape the year we sold our Portland house. I've often seen people maximize their garden space by growing their squash plants over an arbor and then planting lettuce and other delicate veggies underneath.

Don't be afraid to think out of the box and get creative. There's more to squash than the traditional garden plot!

Adding vines to your forest garden can add beauty, attract beneficial insects and birds, and add another food crop. Don't forget to include this important layer!

16 Great Ground Covers For Your Fruit Tree Guild

Adding ground covers to your fruit tree guild is a great idea. While you can add mulch into your food forest, by including a living mulch you are both improving the soil, saving water, and adding in another food crop.

Here are some great ground covers for your food forest:

Chamomile

If you would like to grow Chamomile as a ground cover, make sure you plant the Roman variety. Once established it can be a lawn replacement as it grows from rhizomes. It is lower growing than German Chamomile, which means you won't need to mow it like you would grass.

Both German and Roman Chamomile have a wide variety of uses as a tea. It's classically used for relaxation and encouraging sleep. If you want to save the flowers for medicinal uses, they can be easily dehydrated.

Clover

Clover is a great nitrogen fixer, but it is also useful as a ground cover. You can walk on it, mow it, or cut it back where it grows to increase soil fertility. Plus, bees love it!

Cucumbers

For a short-term ground cover, consider cucumbers. It's a great living mulch for sunny spaces where your trees have not yet grown to cover. Plus, you get to harvest the cucumbers for eating or pickles, then let the vines build the soil at the end of the season.

Hostas

Surprisingly, hostas are edible. You can eat the young shoots like asparagus in the spring. They make a great ground cover because they thrive in shade and last all season long. Plus they will come back year after year!

Melons

Like cucumbers, melons make a great ground cover for those sunny patches between trees. They'll keep your ground protected and you get delicious fruit!

Nasturtium

Nasturtiums are one of the most popular companion plants for vegetables because they attract beneficial insects, repel harmful insects, and are edible themselves! Don't hesitate to add them into any sunny niche.

Oregano

Oregano is one of my favorite ground covers because it is dense and spreads itself, but not overwhelming. It smells nice and holds up well if you need to walk on it, but it doesn't have to be mowed at all. Plus, you can harvest it for use in the kitchen!

Parsley

Like oregano, parsley is a good herb to use when filling in blank spaces in your landscape. It has many culinary uses, and it contains many nutrients. You will need to plant it each year, however.

Peanuts

If you replant every year, you can grow peanuts as a ground cover and as a food crop, but there is also an ornamental peanut plant that can replace lawn. It is perennial and also has an edible flower.

Pumpkins

Like cucumbers and melons, pumpkins will very happily provide a living mulch to cover your ground during the growing season. They like sunshine and lots of space to spread out, but on the plus side you can grow your own jack o'lanterns!

Rhubarb

While rhubarb plants are not traditional ground covers, it generally grows very quickly and doesn't need much water. It will readily spread and grow happily almost anywhere you put it. You can also chop and drop the leaves when you harvest the stalks to mulch in place.

Salad Vegetables

Virtually any salad green can be popped into blank spaces in your garden. They don't need much space to grow. Also, they grow well in shade and are a great way to add another crop when you don't have much available space.

Strawberry

If you want to grow strawberries as a ground cover you have a few options. You can grow any variety, but if you want a lot of runners to cover a lot of ground select a June bearing fruit. If you're filling in a very shady spot wild strawberries are best, particularly the woodland strawberry.

Squash

Need a sunny space filled and quickly? Opt for squash. When we put our house up for sale I filled in blank spaces in our landscape with various squashes. Plus, if you grow winter squash it will store for months in a cool pantry.

Sweet potato

Sweet potatoes grow quickly from stem cuttings and quickly fill in food forests. They will only last one season, but they are a great option for warm weather locations.

Thyme

Like oregano, thyme is a wonderful herb for ground covers. It spreads well, lasts many seasons, is walk-able, and smells great. Plus, you can use it in the kitchen. It goes great in split pea soup!

44 Insectiary Plants For Your Fruit Tree Guild

A vital part of a healthy garden is the insect population. While insects get a bad reputation, many of them are essential for a healthy ecosystem. Here are some insectiary plants that will bene t the "good" bugs or discourage those you don't want around.

Insectiary Plants To Attract Pollinators

Most of us know how important it is to attract pollinators to our fruit trees and gardens. Insectiary plants are the plants that help support beneficial insects. Sometimes that's providing nectar or pollen. Other times it's providing shelter or a host plant for reproduction.

Here are plants that will attract these beneficial insects to your food forest:
- Alyssum
- Aster
- Basil
- Bee Balm
- Borage
- Bronze Fennel
- Calendula
- Chives

- Comfrey
- Cornflowers
- Dahlia
- Daylily
- Delphinium
- Dill
- Echinacea
- Echium
- Fennel
- Fuschia
- Hosta
- Kniphofia
- Laburnum (Golden Chain Tree)
- Lamb's Ear
- Lavender
- Lupine
- Milkweed
- Mint
- Poached Egg Plant
- Salvia
- Sunflowers
- Thyme
- Yarrow

Plants That Repel Pests

While many insects are useful to have in a fruit tree guild or food forest, there are some insects that can cause damage to your crops. Instead of spraying pesticides try planting more plants that will attract their predators. Thankfully, there are also plants that will make those nuisances less likely to settle into your garden as their new home.

Here are 14 insectiary plants that will reduce obnoxious bugs:
- Basil
- Citronella
- Coriander
- Dill
- Fennel
- Garlic/Onion family
- Lavender
- Lemongrass
- Marigold
- Mint
- Nasturtium
- Peppermint
- Sunflower
- Thyme

By making space for as many of these plants as you can in your fruit tree guild you can help create a healthy eco-system within your property. You will have great biodiversity, and your plants will be healthier and happier. Not to mention many of these plants are beautiful too!

What Are The Best Nitrogen Fixers?

Nitrogen fixers are an important part of fruit tree guilds. These plants can also really help out your garden and ornamental plants. Nitrogen fixers are basically self-fertilizing plants. Skip the store-bought fertilizers and grow your own!

What Is Nitrogen Fixation?

Nitrogen fixation is a process where nitrogen is pulled out of the air and made available for use. The industrial process for this is called the Haber-Bosch process. Nitrogen and hydrogen are combined from the air under high pressure and high temperatures with a catalyst to produce ammonia.

I bet you didn't know that your garden is doing a similar chemical process all on its own! The roots of some plants have symbiotic bacteria that live on the nitrogen found in the air. They store it in the plant on nodes on the roots, and then it's released once the plant decays.

Nitrogen is an essential component for healthy plants. If you don't have enough available nitrogen, you may see symptoms of deficiency. These look like yellow, pale green leaves. Nitrogen is abundantly available as a gas, but plants can't use it in that form. So, the bacteria utilize an anaerobic chemical reaction that produces ammonia. Thankfully, that's a form of nitrogen plants can utilize.

Diazotrophs is the name for all nitrogen fixing bacteria in general. However, there are different types. One of the most common nitrogen fixers are the legume family. The symbiotic bacteria that lives with legumes is called *Rhizobium*.

Most gardeners will inoculate legume seeds with *Rhizobium* just in case it isn't present in the soil. *Bradyrhizobium* are other bacteria that are also symbiotic with legumes.

There are other nitrogen fixing bacteria, such as the *Frankia* bacteria, which are present on plants that are members of the rose, birch, and bayberry families. *Azospirillum* is symbiotic with cereal grasses.

One of the most common nitrogen fixing bacteria that does not have a symbiotic relationship is cyanobacteria, algae found in the ocean.

How Do Nitrogen Fixers Work In The Garden?

All that nitrogen that is stored by the symbiotic bacteria builds up in plant tissue. Many people plant a legume cover crop, and then till the plants back into the soil in order to release the nitrogen. A rye grass or clover winter cover crop is a popular option.

For a forest garden, you can also plant perennial nitrogen fixers. Just periodically chop back the leaves above ground and let them decompose in place. The pruning also causes slight root dieback underground, which makes some nitrogen available to other plants.

Some plants store more nitrogen than others, and if you choose plants that store the most you will need to devote less of your space to these plants and can grow more useful plants.

Oftentimes nitrogen fixers are also known as pioneer species. Pioneer species thrive in poor soil and disturbed land. They are sometimes considered invasive, but really, they are taking damaged land, and preparing it for more delicate plants.

There is a very detailed calculator available from the USDA where you can filter by your state and county and pull up lists of suggested plants based on what qualities you are looking for. If you're not sure if a certain plant is okay for your area, this is a great resource.

Multi-use Nitrogen Fixers For Your Food Forest

With all these benefits, you need to plant these highly useful plants in your own yard or forest garden. Here are some great choices organized by other benefits. And the more uses, the more you can do in smaller spaces!

Edible Nitrogen Fixers

All of these plants can be used both to build your soil, but also as a food source.
- Ahipa
- Alfalfa
- American Licorice
- Beans
- Black-eyed Pea
- Breadroot
- Carob
- Chickpea
- Fava Beans
- Goumi
- Ice Cream Bean Tree
- Jicama
- Lentils
- Peanut
- Peas
- Pigeon Pea
- Prairie Acacia
- Sea Buckthorn
- Siberian Pea Shrub
- Silver Birch
- Tamarind

Insectiary Nitrogen Fixers

These plants are host plants or food sources for beneficial insects. And of course, they may be attractive to humans as well!

- Bird's-foot Trefoil
- Black Locust
- Clover
- Comfrey
- False Indigo
- Goumi
- Honey Locust
- Linden Tree
- Lupine
- Silk Tree
- Silver Birch
- Sweet Fern

Ornamental Nitrogen Fixers

Surrounding ourselves with beauty is important too. It's okay for some of our plants to be merely ornamental, and these are still good for the soil.

- Bladder Senna
- Carob
- California Lilac
- Golden Chain Tree
- Honey Locust
- Linden Tree
- Sidebeak Pencil Flower

- Silk Tree
- Silver Birch
- Silver Wattle
- Sweet Pea
- Wisteria
- Yellow Wood Tree

Livestock Feed and Pasture

If you have enough space for pastured livestock, here are some nutritional nitrogen fixers to add into your pasture and browse.

- Alfalfa
- Bird's-foot Trefoil
- Black Locust
- Clover
- Kudzu
- Pigeon Pea
- Siberian Pea Shrub
- Tagasaste
- Vetch

Medicinal

If you are into herbal medicine, here are some plants that may be good to have on hand in addition to their nitrogen fixation abilities.

- Alder
- Alfalfa
- Birch

- Black Locust
- Clover
- Honeybush
- Mountain Mahogany
- Prairie Acacia
- Redbush
- Scotch Broom
- Sea Buckthorn
- Sweetgale
- Tamarind

Other Useful Nitrogen Fixers

- Alder (woodworking)
- American licorice (erosion control)
- Bayberry (good for hedges and birds)
- Birch (woodworking, nurse tree for seedlings, sap)
- Black Locust (woodworking, weed control, erosion control)
- False Indigo (dye)
- Kudzu (prevents erosion, good for basket making)
- Mesquite (woodworking and edible pods)
- Siberian Pea Shrub (good for hedges)
- Tagasaste (good for hedges)
- Mountain Mahogany (Woodworking, medicinal)

Can Be Invasive

These plants grow eagerly and can overtake more delicate native ones, so if you plant them, feel free to prune with gusto. While many people demonize invasive plants, remember that they are often invasive because we have already disturbed and damaged the native ecosystem. These types of plants thrive in and improve poor soils and can be controlled with active management.

- Autumn Olive
- Bird's-foot Trefoil
- Black Locust
- Cape Broom
- Honey Locust
- Kudzu
- Mesquite
- Scotch Broom
- Silk Tree
- Wisteria (non-native types)

There are so many different nitrogen fixers that you should be able to find the perfect ones for your individual needs. Adding in nitrogen fixers is a great way to increase the overall health of your garden, food forest, or yard.

17 Dynamic Accumulators You Need In Your Food Forest

Dynamic accumulators are a popular idea in permaculture. It refers to plants that have deep roots that gather minerals. This is a process called phytoaccumulation, and different plants can accumulate different metals.

The theory is that you plant these deep-rooted plants, they draw up nutrients from deep within the soil. When the plant decomposes it makes those minerals more available for the more shallow-rooted plants.

There isn't much scientific data on if the minerals are broken down and available for other plants, but there are many case studies that show a positive effect.

We do know that some plants are used to clean up land that has been contaminated. Phytoaccumulating plants will gather up the toxins such as lead and can then be buried deep into the ground where they will not injure people.

We also know that many plants thrive with the addition of mulches and compost. Many of these types of plants work great for creating a lot of bulky plant material that you can "chop and drop" in place as mulch. They're also great for adding to the compost when it needs bulked up.

Plus, so many plants have multiple uses! They can be medicinal or edible. They can attract beneficial insects such as bees. And sometimes they can just be beautiful to look at.

Adding more variety of plants on your property, and especially near your trees can help create a vibrant mini ecosystem.

Here are 17 popular dynamic accumulators that you should plant that will benefit your garden and trees:

- Amaranth
- Apple Tree
- Birch Tree
- Borage
- Chickweed
- Chicory
- Comfrey
- Daikon Radish
- Dandelion
- Horsetail
- Lamb's Quarters
- Maple Tree
- Moringa
- Mulberry
- Nettles
- Sorrel
- Yarrow

I look forward to more data being gathered on dynamic accumulators. But I won't be waiting until then before I start planting these useful species in my food forest.

Best Plants To Chop and Drop In Your Fruit Tree Guild

One of the critical aspects of growing a fruit tree guild is that you grow your compost and fertilizer alongside of your fruiting trees and edible

plants. These types of plants are often called mulch plants, and the process of pruning them back is often called "chop and drop."

While you can still make traditional compost, it can be much more effective to simply chop back plants and let them compost in place. It also requires less work on your part. Not only do you save on making and hauling compost, but it also reduces weeding.

Mulcher Plants to Chop and Drop
Alfalfa

Alfalfa is a popular mulch plant, so why not grow your own! It is a nitrogen fixer and drought tolerant. Its roots can reach up to 20 feet to break up hard soil. When you cut it back those roots will decompose, leaving your soil more aerated.

It's also great for bees, and nutritious for humans as well. You can also dry it and turn it into a powder to use as a fertilizer.

Artichoke

Artichokes are fun to eat and delicious. Plus, they're easy to grow in your food forest. They are related to sunflowers and dandelions and make great mulch plants. Let your plants grow all spring, and after the last harvest, cut the plants back. Mulch them well for winter, and they will come back in the spring.

Barberry

Barberry can be invasive in some areas, so check before you plant it. The fruit is technically edible but not sweet. There are some medicinal uses. Barberry makes a good privacy hedge, especially with its long thorns. You can chop it all the way back to the base and it will regrow. So, chop and drop to your heart's content!

Borage

Borage is a wonderful option for chop and drop mulches. It has edible and attractive flowers and attracts bees. It repels cabbage worms and makes a great companion plant in the vegetable garden.

It is an annual, but it should self-seed itself. You can also cut back the stems when they get leggy to encourage regrowth. Plus, once it's established it can handle hot, dry weather.

You can make a poultice or tea with the leaves, which have high levels of calcium and potassium. You can plant it as a companion plant, cover crop, or chicken feed, and when it's over for the season, simply leave it in place as a mulch.

Buckwheat

Buckwheat makes a good cover crop as it grows quickly. It can be ready to chop into mulch in as little as 30 days. It's good for people and chickens love it. Or if you don't need it as a mulch, just let some go to seed to attract beneficial insects.

Comfrey

Comfrey tends grows big, so all you need to do is cut back leaves and leave them in place. In just a couple weeks it will start to grow back. Just be sure about where you want to plant it, because once it's established it is really hard to kill. This tenacity means that you can chop and drop your comfrey multiple times a year.

Comfrey is also called knitbone and can be used in poultices. Bees love its pretty flowers and it is very easy to propagate from root cuttings. A good idea is to plant one at the base of each fruit tree for easy mulching. Plus, in hot summers it will appreciate a touch of shade, while getting full sun during the colder times of the year.

Jerusalem Artichoke

Jerusalem Artichoke is an edible tuber will return year after year even after you harvest it. The pretty yellow flowers resemble wild sunflowers, and it will grow just about anywhere. Chickens will eat the shoots, but if left alone it can grow to as tall as ten feet. If you want to harvest the tubers you can cut it down to four feet tall and mulch with the cuttings. Or if you aren't planning to eat the tubers, use the plant as mulch over the winter.

If you do want to eat the tubers, start harvesting after frost. They won't last long once they're harvested but the tubers will wait in the ground to be harvested. If you want even larger tubers the next year, dig up as many as you can and replant the biggest and smoothest ones.

Laburnum (Or Golden Chain)

This poisonous tree has beautiful flowers and is often grown as an ornamental. It is a member of the pea family (but don't eat it!), which makes it a good choice for encouraging soil fertility when used as a mulch.

Traditionally it has been used for fence posts, and occasionally will re-sprout and grow. It can be coppiced, makes good firewood, and the wood is also used for instruments and furniture.

Licorice

Licorice is also a member of the pea family, and unlike Labernum, has a long history of being used in the kitchen! It also has a long history of medicinal uses.

Licorice is not a quick acting plant so pick something else for short term mulches. It will take 3-4 years until the roots are harvestable. It will grow to about 3-4 feet tall and is drought tolerant after the first year. Dig up the roots after the third year to harvest. Just make sure to keep some aside for replanting, then use the plant material as a mulch.

Nasturtium

Nasturtium is a versatile plant. The entire plant is edible and high in minerals and nutrients. It also has a history of medicinal uses. Nasturtiums make a great living mulch and weed barrier, plus the bees love it. It is beautiful and easy to grow. It can be used to fill holes in the landscape, as a companion plant to deter pests, as a ground cover or vine, and will tolerate being chopped and dropped well.

Rhubarb

Rhubarb stalks are fun to cook with, but the leaves are poisonous. When you are harvesting the stalks make sure to pull o the leaves. You can then put them back under the plant or used in a different area of the garden. Rhubarb can also grow enthusiastically and will handle being harvested and cut back.

Stinging Nettles

You may not want to intentionally plant stinging nettles in a small yard, but they are highly useful if they are growing on your property. Stinging nettles are good to eat once they are cooked.

Nettles are incredibly nutritious both for people and soils. You can chop them and let them break down in place, make fertilizer with them, or even just add them into your compost bins.

By growing your own mulch plants, you will save money, time and e ort! You can chop and drop just about any plant, but these will really bene t your soil and help keep the weeds down.

The Most Common Challenges To Starting A Fruit Tree Guild

There are many great reasons to plant a fruit tree guild. Why might people not take advantage of all the benefits? What can cause challenges to starting your fruit guild?

Common Challenges For Fruit Tree Guilds

There are several common problems that many people have run into. By far the most common is planting your trees too close together. I am guilty of this, and so are many, many others. But what other obstacles should you look out for?

What IS a fruit tree guild?

The first and biggest issue is a lack of common knowledge! While fruit tree guilds are very popular in permaculture literature, they have yet to permeate into colloquial knowledge. If more people were introduced to the idea, we could have higher producing backyard orchards, and take advantage of already established fruit trees.

If you haven't heard of a fruit tree guild or food forest before, think of it as companion plants for perennial plants! Instead of having a fruit tree standing alone in the grass, plant other species around it to bene t it. Pollinator plants, fertilizer plants, and plants that won't compete for nutrients are all great choices.

Not Enough Time

Like most hobbies, we try to squish our gardening into the nooks and crannies of our busy lives. Between jobs, family, and home it seems like we're running non-stop! It does take time to start out with fruit tree guilds. It takes time to plan what you want to put in. It takes time to nd the best spots for planting. And of course, it takes time to get plants established.

However, the super awesome thing about food forests is that once you put in the time to get them established, they take less and less time. A maturing fruit tree guild should require less time treating disease or needing fertilized. It will need less weeding. It will certainly take less time than starting seeds and planting an annual vegetable garden.

If you've set it up properly, you should be able to spend very little time besides some annual pruning and harvesting!

Not Enough Space (Or Too Much!)

The trickiest part of planning a fruit tree guild is knowing where to put everything and planning it all out. You can actually make some very tiny guilds. Some people have used columnar apple trees or dwarf fruit trees to put a fruit tree guild in areas as small as side yards. If you really have no space, plant a potted tree and include some herbs in the pot with it.

But on the flip side, the most common mistake people make is planting trees too close together. This is true even for those with larger properties.

If you have a small property stick to dwarf or semi dwarf trees. You may even only have room for one! If you have more space, I think that makes it trickier because there's so much planning that needs done.

I believe the best place to start is one step at a time. Either get all your trees into the ground right away so they can start maturing or take it one fruit tree at a time and get the entire guild established. Just don't try to do everything all at once!

I recommend starting closest to your home and working out from there. It will be easiest to maintain if it's closer to you. You'll be able to notice what's growing well and what's not without a lot of e ort.

I also recommend starting with plans for a specific guild to start with instead of trying to create your own. Creating your own is great fun, but it can be a bit overwhelming.

Too Much Digging!

Digging holes is seriously a downside of planting fruit trees. Depending on what the soil is like in your area and your own strength it could be downright impossible!

If you are a decently strong individual, I recommend a post hole digger. These take quite a bit of effort but go much more quickly than a shovel. If you have quite a bit of rock, you may want to look into a digging bar.

Another option is to rent a jackhammer. Most cities have tool rental places nearby where you can rent equipment by the hour. We have done this in the past and it's very handy and much cheaper than trying to buy something we'll only need for a weekend!

If you just can't get the tools you need, consider planting dwarf varieties in pots. You can add many other beneficial plants in raised beds on your property as well.

We once had an older neighbor with a gorgeous yard. For years she was out there working on it herself, but near the end of her life she just wasn't physically able to do all the work it required. She hired someone to come out periodically and do the heavy digging and other large projects for her.

There is no shame in hiring help to get your fruit tree guilds established.

Getting Your Partner on Board

Like any homesteading endeavor (or life endeavor, really!) it's super-duper important that your partner is willing to give it a try. Compromises are a great way to start. Perhaps your partner is nervous about messy fruit trees. Instead you could start out with some medicinal guilds. Or maybe you keep a traditional yard close to the house, and establish a guild on the edge of your property

Another option is to try something on a very small scale and share the benefits with those you care about. Perhaps a garden bed can be transformed into a mini guild, before applying those principles on a larger scale. Citrus in a container is a very non-messy fruit option for warmer climates. The fruit will stay on the tree until harvested.

What Do I Plant?

Knowing what to plant is a big problem for many of us! There are SO MANY options!

The good news is, there are no hard and fast rules. You can experiment if you'd like. If you plant something and it doesn't do well, learn from it and try something new. And if your plants thrive, GREAT!

When deciding where to purchase plants, keep in mind your climate. Local varieties from local nurseries will most likely do better than those mail ordered from a completely different zone, or plants that are shipped to the entire country.

Keeping It All Straight

Sometimes we just feel like there are too many balls in the air at one time. We have the best of intentions, but not the skills or knowledge we need. This is when having great resources available makes a huge difference.

For example, one of my favorite tree care books is Pruning Made Easy by Lewis Hill. I can't keep all those nitty gritty details straight in my head, so great reference materials are an absolute must.

This is also a great reason to take things slowly and put in one guild at a time instead of trying to plant everything all at once. This way you get to learn what each individual tree needs before adding in others.

There is so much to learn that if we waited until we had everything perfect before we started, we'd never get going at all! Even if you've run into some roadblocks with your food forests, keep trying! Even slow progress is worth taking the time, so don't let yourself get discouraged if you run into challenges.

The best thing you can do is to start experimenting with your plants and climate and learn what works the best for your needs. Don't be afraid to make mistakes, especially after you have taken the time to prepare and learn about the plants you plan to include in your fruit tree guilds.

Printed in Great Britain
by Amazon